I Wonder How God Made Me

Mona Gansberg Hodgson

Illustrated by Chris Sharp

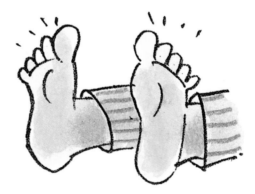

CPH
SAINT LOUIS

For Jared and Hannah Knister and all children—they are
precious in God's sight

I Wonder Series

I Wonder How Fish Sleep
I Wonder Who Hung the Moon in the Sky
I Wonder Who Stretched the Giraffe's Neck
I Wonder How God Hears Me
I Wonder How God Made Me
I Wonder What I Can Give God

All Scripture quotations, unless otherwise indicated, are taken from the HOLY BIBLE, NEW INTERNATIONAL VERSION®.
NIV®. Copyright © 1973, 1978, 1984 by International Bible Society. Used by permission of Zondervan Publishing
House. All rights reserved.

Text copyright © 1999 Mona Gansberg Hodgson
Art copyright © 1999 Concordia Publishing House
Published by Concordia Publishing House
3558 S. Jefferson Avenue, St. Louis, MO 63118-3968
Manufactured in the United States of America

2   3   4   5   6   7   8   9   10   11   10   09   08   07   06   05   04   03   02   01

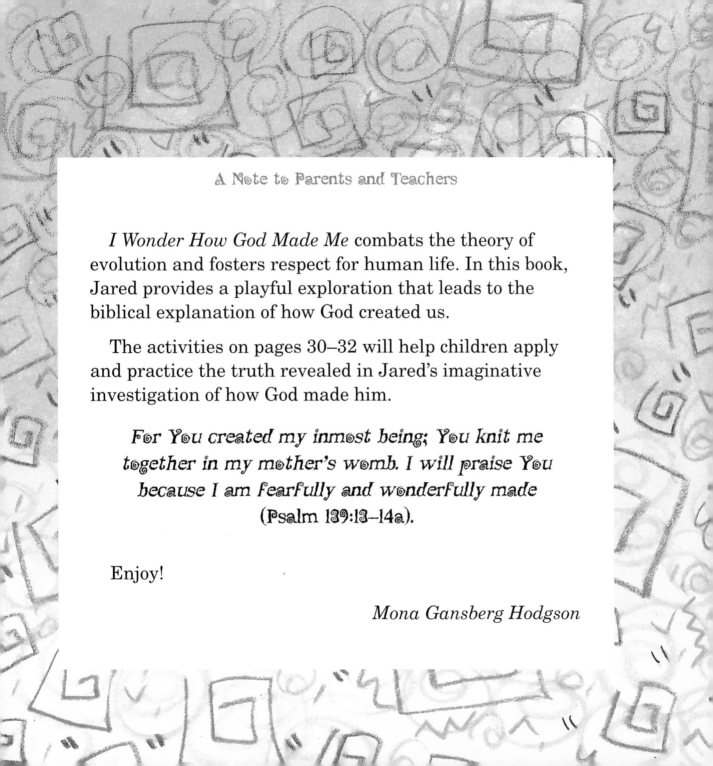

A Note to Parents and Teachers

I Wonder How God Made Me combats the theory of evolution and fosters respect for human life. In this book, Jared provides a playful exploration that leads to the biblical explanation of how God created us.

The activities on pages 30–32 will help children apply and practice the truth revealed in Jared's imaginative investigation of how God made him.

For You created my inmost being; You knit me together in my mother's womb. I will praise You because I am fearfully and wonderfully made (Psalm 139:13–14a).

Enjoy!

Mona Gansberg Hodgson

Hi! My name is Jared. I live in Arizona. Where do you live?

Do you ever wonder about things? I do. Everything I see makes me wonder. I like to wonder. Do you like to wonder too?

od made the earth. God
made the sky. We can read all
about it in the Bible. Papa Ray
says God also made me. And He
made you too. Isn't God amazing?

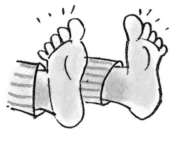

This morning when I wiggled my toes and scratched my nose, I began to wonder. Can you guess what I wondered?

How did God make me? How did God make you? I wonder!

Mad Dog!

When I helped my mom make cookies, we put lots of stuff in the bowl: eggs, flour, butter, and my favorite—chocolate chips! Then we put blobs of the dough on cookie sheets. When the oven timer rang, we had cookies!

DING

Do you think God stirred a bunch of things together and made *us* out of cookie dough or bread dough? I wonder.

When bread gets old it turns green with mold. I don't think God made us out of dough. I'm not moldy, are you?

My dad and Papa Ray made signs for kids to paint. They mixed plaster and water and poured it into plastic molds. When the plaster hardened, we all had signs that read, "God is amazing!"

I wonder if God mixed stuff together and made us in a mold. What do you think?

My dad says God made each one of us special. We are all different, so I don't think God used a mold to make us.

BOY-OH-BOY

EYE COLOR:
BROWN

HAIR COLOR:
BLACK

E ↑ F

13

Have you ever played with squishy clay? I like to push it into different shapes like trees, or dogs, or birds.

Everything I make with clay looks different. I make it special. Do you think maybe God shaped us out of clay? I wonder.

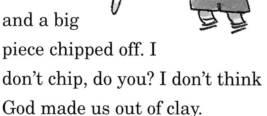

My sister dropped one of my clay creations and a big piece chipped off. I don't chip, do you? I don't think God made us out of clay.

Papa Ray whittles lots of different things out of wood. He made a doll for my sister. Right now he is whittling a whistle for me.

I wonder if God likes to whittle. Do you think God carved us out of wood?

Papa Ray says that wood doesn't have a brain, so wood can't think. I know God gave us a brain so we can think and learn more about Him. I don't think God made us out of wood.

17

My family goes to the mountains in the wintertime to play in the snow. We like to make snowmen.

I wonder if God packed and stacked snow to make us. What do you think?

We'd melt in the summer if we were made out of snow! I don't melt. Do you? I don't think God made us out of snow.

I saw a robot on TV. Robots move, and each one is different. And robots won't melt in the sun.

Did God build us with mechanical parts, like a robot? I wonder.

What do you think?

My dad says that a robot doesn't have a heart. I know God gave us a heart so we can love Him. I don't think God made us like a robot.

In Genesis 2:7, the Bible says that God breathed into Adam's nostrils. My dad blew up balloons for my sister's birthday party. He puffed air into the balloons and they grew bigger and bigger. I am getting bigger. Does God puff air into me and blow me up like a balloon? I wonder.

Some balloons pop when they are poked. Not me. I know God breathes life into us, but we are not like balloons.

23

I know God didn't make me out of cookie dough or out of snow.

I know God didn't make me like a robot. I am a person and so are you.

The Bible says God formed all my parts while my mom was pregnant and I was growing inside her. God was getting me ready to be born. WOW! God is so-o-o-o amazing! How God made me is wonderful. And how He made you is wonderful too!

I like to wonder, don't you?

When I wonder, I think about God. I like to think about God. I like to thank God for making me. I like to thank Him for giving me a heart so I can love Him.

Thank You, God, for making me.
Thank You for caring about me
    before I was born.
Thank You for caring about me now.
And thank You, God, for sending
    Jesus so I can live forever
    in heaven.
Thank You for being
    my amazing God!
In Jesus' name.
    Amen.

For You created my inmost being;
You knit me together in my
mother's womb. I will praise You
because I am fearfully and
wonderfully made.
(Psalm 139:13–14a)

29

31

What do you like best about the way God made you? Tell me about it in the space below.